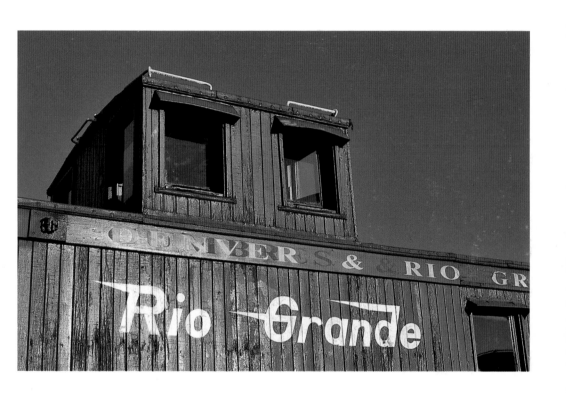

D1295641

Caboose

by Brian Solomon

Voyageur Press

First published in 2011 by Voyageur Press, an imprint of MBI Publishing Company, 400 First Avenue North, Suite 300, Minneapolis, MN 55401 USA

Voyageur Press titles are also available at discounts in bulk quantity for industrial or sales-promotional use. For details write to Special Sales Manager at MBI Publishing Company, 400 First Avenue North, Suite 300, Minneapolis, MN 55401 USA.

To find out more about our books, visit us online at www.voyageurpress.com.

Front cover: Grand Trunk Western 77136 works with an Alco S-4 switcher in Detroit, Michigan, in August 1968. Despite its age at the time of this photograph, this old wooden-bodied caboose was maintained in excellent condition. *George W. Kowanski*

Frontispiece: Rio Grande continued to operate traditional wooden-bodied cabooses on its narrow gauge lines in Colorado and New Mexico for years after steel cabooses were the norm on its standard gauge lines. *Brian Solomon*

Title pages: Conrail's Buffalo Division caboose, photographed at Churchville, New York, in 1987, was covered with slogans and witticisms. This end of the caboose read: "The Best SAFETY DEVICE is . . . You." The opposite end read: "Is this the END? No, the Beginning." *Brian Solomon*

Editor: Dennis Pernu
Design Manager: LeAnn Kuhlmann
Layout: Jennie Tischler

Printed in China

Library of Congress Cataloging-in-Publication Data

Solomon, Brian, 1966–
  Caboose / Brian Solomon.
     p. cm.
  Includes index.
  ISBN 978-0-7603-3942-8 (sb : alk. paper)
  1. Cabooses (Railroads) I. Title.
  TF485.S55 2011
  625.2'2--dc22

                              2010031644

Contents

Acknowledgments

Growing up in the late 1970s and early 1980s, I was fortunate to experience caboose operations when virtually every North American railroad routinely assigned cabooses to freights. The sight of a caboose bobbing along behind a long string of cars accompanied by the friendly wave from a conductor or brakeman was part of everyday railroading. Thanks to the generosity of railroaders, I had the privilege to enjoy the thrills of riding a caboose first-hand. My first caboose trip was in an antique wooden-bodied car on Maine's Belfast & Moosehead Lake Railroad in August 1980. My father, Richard Jay Solomon, and I rode from Belfast to the Maine Central interchange at Burnham Junction. Subsequently, I rode cabooses on Conrail and Southern Pacific, and have had the opportunity to experience preserved cars on a host of tourist railways, including Iowa's Boone & Scenic Valley, New York's Adirondack Scenic Railroad, and the now defunct Kettle Moraine in Wisconsin.

This book wouldn't have been possible if not for many railroaders who opened doors along the way. Special thanks to Robert Foreman at Conrail, Adirondack Scenic General Manager Thomas L. Carver, Bob Hoppe and J. D. Schmid at SP, Jim Beagle at Central Vermont, Richard Gruber of Wisconsin & Southern, Bob Bentley of Mass Central, Dave Swirk and all the employees of the Pioneer Valley Railroad, Joe Burgess and Gary Gilbert at Amtrak, Howard Pincus of the Railroad Museum of New England, and Dan Bigda of Boxcar Services.

John Gruber and I wrote a more comprehensive text on cabooses commissioned by Andover Junction and published by MBI Publishing Company in 2001. Research John did for that book aided this effort. Bob Buck of Tucker's Hobbies in Warren, Massachusetts, has encouraged me for many years and has always conveyed his knowledge to me with enthusiasm and accuracy. Bob has loaned me some of his excellent period work for this book as well as a variety of images from his collection. Doug Eisele and David Monte Verde of Genesee Valley Transportation assisted with captions. Rich Reed advised me on the particulars of Pennsylvania Railroad, New York Central, Penn-Central, and Conrail cabooses. Russell Buck assisted with research on Burlington Northern's cabooses.

In the course of making photos over the years, many fellow photographers have traveled with me, guiding my interest and advising me on technique, locations, and operations. Among these are Brian L. Jennison, Mel Patrick, Michael L. Gardner, T. S. Hoover, George S. Pitarys, Tim Doherty, Pat Yough, Mike Abalos, Dean Sauvola, Tom Danneman, Mike Danneman, John Gruber, Dick Gruber, Chris Burger, Scott Bontz, Phil Brahms, Justin Tognetti, Kevin Dorn, Blair Kooistra, Mark Hemphill, Brian Rutherford, Joe McMillan, Don Gulbrandsen, Joe Snopek, Dan Munson, Doug Moore, Mike Schafer, Otto Vondrak, Dave Burton, Don Marson, Gerald Hook, Danny Johnson, F. L. Becht, Ed Beaudette, George C. Corey, Howard Ande, Brandon Delaney, Mark Leppert, Bill Linley, George Melvin, Chris Guss, Marshall Beecher, Tim Hensch, Dan Howard, Vic Neves, Emile Tobenfeld, Will Holloway, Hal Miller, John Peters, Norman Yellin, my father, Richard Jay Solomon, and my brother, Seán Solomon.

Thanks are owed to contributing photographers for loaning images to this project, each of whom are credited alongside their work herein: George W. Kowanski, Jim Shaughnessy, Patrick Yough, Bill Vigrass, Jay Williams, Brian L. Jennison, Thomas L. Carver, George S. Pitarys, John Leopard, Scott Muskopf, Tom Kline, Dennis LeBeau, Nick and Rich Zmijewski, Thomas Figura, Keith Sirman of the Sirman Collection, and Richard Jay Solomon.

Thanks also go to my mother, Maureen Solomon, who has taken a keen interest in my photography, sometimes seeing details in photographs I may have missed. This book would be just loose photographs and words if it weren't for my editor, Dennis Pernu, and everyone at Voyageur Press for putting together the book you hold in your hands.

Although this is a completed volume, the research and photography have been ongoing for decades. I've made an effort to select photographs that work together, while trying to weave themes of interest into the captions. Please enjoy!

On August 30, 1987, old Maine Central cabooses rest in Boston & Maine's East Deerfield Yard near Greenfield, Massachusetts. Their useful life is over and these classic cars are probably making their final journey. Maine Central maintained an eclectic fleet of cabooses right to the end of caboose operations, including cars such as 614R, which featured plywood siding. *Brian Solomon*

Introduction

In the mid- to late nineteenth century, the caboose emerged as a crucial type of rolling stock on North American railways. The romance associated with railroaders and railway travel has made it an iconic symbol of American freight railroading. Unlike the locomotive, which has been carefully chronicled and documented in exceptional detail, the early history of the caboose remains shrouded in lore. It is understood that an antecedent to the caboose was the "conductor's car," credited to the vision of an industrious freight conductor on New York's Auburn & Syracuse. In the mid-1840s, A&S converted a surplus boxcar into an office and tool car, establishing a precedent for a crew car at the back of the train.

By the 1860s, the conductor's car had found numerous applications as railroads began to separate freight and passenger traffic and run longer, heavier freights.

In those days, before the invention and widespread application of the automatic airbrake, train brakes were set by hand. On passenger trains, conductor and brakemen could walk from car to car in order to set and release brakes. This was not possible with freight trains, so cars were equipped with catwalks and grab irons that allowed trainmen to walk from car to car while the train was in motion. Freight train speeds in those times were still relatively slow—often little more than 12 miles per hour—yet the brakeman's job was perilous, especially in inclement weather. As trains grew longer, more brakemen were required and the logistics of train operations grew more complex, necessitating a place for crewmembers to ride. Cabooses became common in freight operations after the Civil War, and by the 1870s were virtually universal on every large railroad.

Opposite: A caboose brings up the tail of Central Vermont Railway freight 444 as it rolls southward across the Conrail diamond in Palmer, Massachusetts, in late July 1986. A few days earlier Conrail began its single tracking of the old Boston & Albany route and lifted one of the two main tracks between Palmer and Springfield. The ruins of the old westward main can be seen in the foreground. *Brian Solomon*

The car evolved as a combination observation post, rolling operations center, crew bunk, canteen, conductor's office, and tool car. It was here that a conductor would do his paperwork and manage train operations, while brakemen and flagmen set brakes and protected the back of the train when stopped or waiting in sidings to meet other trains.

The name is unusual. It would appear *caboose* derived from a Dutch word—variously spelled "kabuis" or "kombuis"—describing a small room on a sailing ship used for preparing meals. "Caboose," as it is spelled in English, seems to come into general usage during the mid–eighteenth century, and the Oxford Dictionary cites a marine reference from that period. In their formative years, American railroads adapted words (and practices) from both military and marine vocabulary, so although the word seems odd today, it may have been a logical transferral at the time it was adopted. The freight train, like the sailing ship before it, emerged as a self-sufficient transport entity, and its crews were expected to take care of themselves in the course of their duties.

As its name implies, the caboose was a place to cook, which in the early days was among one of the car's primary functions. In the nineteenth century, before the advent of federally mandated "hours of service" laws, it was common for railroaders to remain on the road for 16 hours or more without scheduled rest. Since many lines served remote territories where there was a dearth of eateries, the caboose's cook stove and stores were needed to feed the crew. Caboose cuisine is a legendary topic of railroad lore—the men out on the road proved creative with their ingredients.

The role of the caboose evolved over the years. In the golden age of American railroads, crews were assigned a specific car that they would make their own. Often this caboose would be taken off a freight at the end of a crew's run and parked on a siding, where they would sleep and prepare meals until their return run. After World War I, railroads moved away from this practice and instead housed operating crews away from their home terminals at company-maintained bunkhouses or in trackside hotels. By the mid–twentieth century most cabooses were assigned to general freight pools and no longer were the domains of specific crews. In most instances cabooses tended to remain on their home roads, but the advent of run-through freights (common by the 1970s) resulted in cabooses roaming offline.

Wide-scale implementation of radio and computer technologies between the 1960s and 1980s, combined with the introduction of innovations such as line-side defect detectors, contributed to the decline of once crucial roles held by the caboose, yet the cars survived under the old work rules. The

Opposite: Grand Trunk Western's end-cupola steel-body caboose 75007 has been preserved at the passenger station in Lapeer, Michigan. Today, GTW lines are operated by parent company Canadian National and caboose operations are just a memory. *Brian Solomon*

A classic Nickel Plate Road caboose marks the back of a steam-hauled freight in the late 1950s. Unlike other freight cars, the caboose has captured a place in the American imagination. *J. William Vigrass*

advent of radio telemetry devices that could monitor brake-pipe pressure at the back of the train, along with greater investment in technologies such as centralized traffic control and reduced crew sizes, combined with revised work rules implemented during the 1980s, resulted in North American railroads phasing out routine caboose operations. Most railroads stopped ordering new cabooses by about 1980. By the mid-1990s, the once common caboose was rapidly becoming an operational anomaly. Today, a few survive in service, but these tend to be used in unusual circumstances where it is necessary to provide a safe place for crews to ride at the back of train.

Opposite: In the 1970s and 1980s Union Pacific was famous for bold slogans emblazoned on the sides of its cabooses. *Brian Solomon*

Chapter 1

Classics

Classics

Although "caboose" was the car's most common name, and certainly the name most recognized by the general public, it was by no means a universal name on North American railroads. In Britain, a similar type of car was called the "brake van." It rode at the back of a freight to assist crews with braking loose-coupled cars in the days before automatic brakes were standard equipment. Canadian railroads developed under British influence. There, cabooses were often known simply as "vans." A few U.S. lines also called them vans.

Of the numerous monikers for the caboose over the years, most undoubtedly originated with the crews. Many are descriptive, and some are derogatory yet repeated so often that they stuck. A four-wheeler might be known as a "bone-shaker," and the old converted boxcar as a "crummy" or a "hack." Some names reflected the hazardous nature of caboose travel. In the days when one of the most dreaded accidents on the railroad was the rear-end collision—an accident that often killed the train's conductor when his caboose was crushed

from behind by a speeding train—some railroaders called the caboose a hearse.

One common descriptive name was cabin or cabin car, which infers the caboose's function: a rolling cabin for crews. The largest railroad to use the cabin car designation was Pennsylvania Railroad, the self-proclaimed "Standard Railroad of the World." Many lines used the term "way car," likely derived from the common way freight—a freight train that made frequent stops along the way to gather and distribute freight cars. As the way freight worked industries and yards en route, its brakemen and flagmen would get on and off the caboose to assist with switching, and to protect the rear of the train from following movements.

The caboose conjures images of red cabooses rolling along with a conductor or brakeman riding in the cupola, a diligent eye cast forward watching for sticking brakes, hotboxes (overheated journal bearings that could result in a derailment), dragging equipment, and other problems. In fact not all cabooses carried cupolas, and a great many were not red. When the cupola was first adopted remains unclear, but by 1900 it was standard equipment. In the early days, cupolas were known as "lookouts" or "observatories;" the word *cupola* was not commonly used until after the turn of the nineteenth century, and on some lines, such as Boston & Maine, they were known as "monitors." Many early cupolas were small, narrow structures that did not span the full width of the car. Later cabooses accommodated full-width cupola designs.

The cupola's inherent advantages as an observatory encouraged railroads to adopt it for most cabooses designed for through-freight service. Added elevation gave the conductor a better forward view of the train while alleviating the risks from leaning out of a window. In addition, his view allowed him to keep an eye on his brakemen for their safety, but also to make sure they were doing their jobs.

The caboose was typically placed at the very back of the train, yet this wasn't always the case. In situations where a rear-end helper was required to push a train up a heavy grade, the caboose was often placed behind the helper engine rather than in front of it. Only with the development of heavy steel-frame cabooses was it deemed safe to place the caboose ahead of the helper. In other situations, a railroad might find it most economical to combine two freight trains en route, which might result in a caboose in the middle of the consist, as well as one at the end. Because of the nature of switching moves along the line, it wasn't always possible or practical to keep the caboose at the end of way freights. So, during portions of the run, the caboose might be found in the middle of the train or even placed directly behind the engine. On "deadhead" moves, when a crew was assigned to move an engine from one terminal to another without freight cars, the engine might run "cab-hop"—just the engine and caboose. In other situations cabooses might congregate at one end of the line as a result of an imbalance in traffic, and thus might be sent back en masse or in groups, resulting in several cabooses at the end of a freight.

A little girl gets the thrill of riding in the cupola of Wisconsin's Kettle Moraine Railway caboose No. 1 as it rolls across a high wooden-pile trestle on June 30, 1996. This popular tourist railway shut its operations in 2001 following opposition from unsympathetic neighbors. *Brian Solomon*

On a frosty afternoon in February 1970, a Bangor & Aroostook wooden-bodied caboose rests near the pier at Searsport, Maine. On some lines, wooden cabooses survived for more than 60 years after the introduction of all-steel designs. *Brian Jennison*

Central of Georgia wooden-bodied caboose X51 is at the back of its freight at Charleston, South Carolina. An estimated 15,000 cabooses were in service on American railroads in 1968. By the time this photo was taken on September 5, 1970, that number was already trending downward. *George W. Kowanski*

Delaware & Hudson 35945 was a wooden-bodied caboose with an end cupola. D&H also had cabooses of a similar design using central cupolas. Significantly, this caboose is equipped with train radio, a relatively unusual innovation for a wooden-bodied car. Notice the diagonal outside metal bracing at the ends. *Jim Shaughnessy*

D&H conductor Jim Morrow and brakeman Walt Benjamine work aboard D&H 35832 at Tahawus, New York. The caboose served as a bunk, canteen, observatory, and office. Although the radio betrays the relatively late date of 1957, in all other respects this view depicts typical life on board a caboose in earlier eras. *Jim Shaughnessy*

In the dead of night on December 6, 1957, D&H brakeman Walt Benjamine radios the head-end crew sitting aboard the engines 85 cars ahead of his caboose. The train will begin its journey from the iron and titanium mine at Tahawus to North Creek, New York. By the late 1950s, portable radios had simplified railroad operations. Advances in radio communications would contribute to the elimination of cabooses on most freights. *Jim Shaughnessy*

Virginia & Truckee No. 24 is a steel-frame, wooden-bodied, off-center cupola caboose that originally served as Nevada Copper Belt No. 24. It was photographed at Carson City, Nevada, on April 15, 1949. *The Sirman Collection*

Wabash 2152 would have been an unusual caboose even at the time it was photographed at Forest, Illinois, in April 1940. Notice the curved rooftop on the cupola, the outside bracing, and the large sliding side door. *The Sirman Collection*

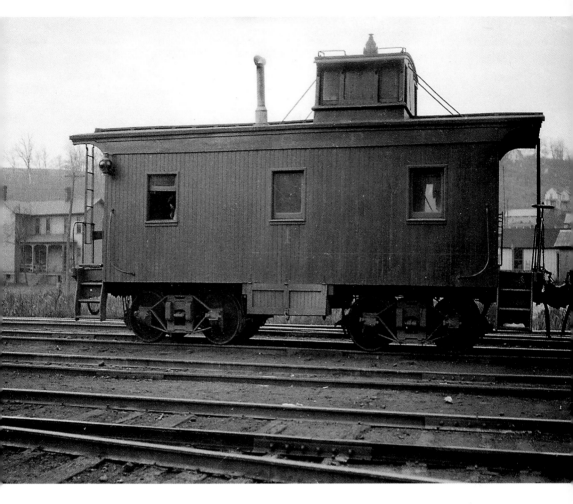

In the nineteenth and early twentieth centuries most railroads used distinctively designed cabooses, leading to considerable variation from road to road, and sometimes even between operating divisions. Buffalo, Rochester & Pittsburg caboose No. 1 is pictured on the back of a coal train at East Salamanca, New York, in about 1920. *The Sirman Collection*

Soo Line operated mixed train services on remote portions of its system. These trains were listed in the public timetable, giving passengers the opportunity to experience a real working railroad for a cash fare. Although the schedules were not especially expedient, the trips were often memorable. *Richard Jay Solomon*

A lone coach and caboose sit in front of the Soo Line depot at Trout Lake, Michigan. This is part of the consist for a mixed freight that will work westward toward Gladstone. In the yard just beyond the depot, the locomotives are switching the freight cars that will make up the rest of the train. Notice the unusual train order signal, a single green light above the door. This depot survives, although Trout Lake is a much quieter place today than it was in 1961. *Richard Jay Solomon*

On this Soo Line mixed consist, the passenger car rode behind the freight cars but ahead of the caboose. The arrangement sometimes gave passengers an unusual forward view, such as this one taken in 1961 of a gondola loaded with freshly cut logs. The ride was aromatic if uneventful. *Richard Jay Solomon*

Restored Soo Line caboose and former Northern Pacific 4-6-0 No. 328 working for the Minnesota Transportation Museum are turned on the wye at Osceola, Wisconsin, on August 17, 1996. *Brian Solomon*

Looking like a scene from decades earlier, Northern Pacific No. 328 and an old Soo Line caboose work an excursion in August 1996. *Brian Solomon*

Well-restored Soo Line wooden-bodied caboose 99103 is displayed at Ladysmith, Wisconsin, along with other historic Soo Line equipment, including an Electro-Motive FP7 diesel. *Thomas L. Carver*

Above: Chesapeake & Ohio's main line was a virtual conveyor belt for Appalachian bituminous. C&O 90813 rolls along on extra 1607 West across the Jackson River Bridge at Clifton Forge, Virginia, on May 11, 1948. Notice the prominent rain guards over the side windows. *Bruce Fales photo, Jay Williams collection*

Opposite top: Atlantic Coast Line 0360 rolls northward past a semaphore serving as a grade-crossing signal. Though the vast majority of semaphores—both electric and mechanical—were used to control train operations, this one is used to warn motorists. Notice the shield to hide the "stop" warning when the blade is in the upright position. More conventional grade-crossing flashers are in place to the right of the semaphore but not yet in service. *Photographer unknown, author collection*

Opposite bottom: ACL connected Richmond, Virginia, with the Carolinas, Georgia, Alabama, and Florida. Caboose 040 is a steel-framed, wooden-bodied type typical of those used on the railroad in the mid–twentieth century. Built in April 1927, it was more than 30 years old at the time of this photograph. *Photographer unknown, author collection*

Canada's Temiskaming & Northern Ontario was the predecessor to the modern-day Ontario Northland. Steel-bodied caboose No. 92 is pictured at New Liskeard on the north shore of Lake Temiskaming on July 18, 1947. *Jim Adams photo, The Sirman Collection*

Ontario Northland wooden-bodied end-cupola caboose No. 70 is seen at North Bay in June 1953. ONR maintained its predecessor's tradition of printing a slogan in an oval on the side of its cabooses. *Ben Cutler photo, The Sirman Collection*

Toronto, Hamilton & Buffalo No. 61 is lined up with other cabooses at Aberdeen Yard in Hamilton, Ontario, on July 14, 1946. *Jim Platt photo, The Sirman Collection*

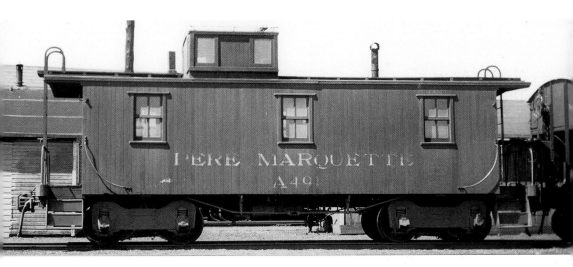

Pere Marquette was a Michigan-based railroad that operated a route across southern Ontario to Buffalo and Niagara Falls. Chesapeake & Ohio acquired it in 1947. In a photo at Port Huron, Michigan, on August 31, 1947, caboose A491 features Fox trucks, a popular style used on steam locomotive tenders and sometimes on cabooses in the early twentieth century. *The Sirman Collection*

New York Central 17854 rolls across a diamond in August 1964. Despite ordering large numbers of steel bay-window cabooses, New York Central continued to employ traditional wooden-bodied, cupola-style cars well into the 1960s. *Richard Jay Solomon*

This New York Central wooden-bodied, end-cupola caboose has been shopped and painted in light gray and scarlet at the Despatch Shops in East Rochester, New York, for the Central's new less-than-carload (LCL) express service marketed as the *Pacemaker*. The railroad reintroduced dedicated fast LCL freight in May 1946, initially connecting New York City and Buffalo and intermediate points. *The Sirman Collection*

New York Central leased the Boston & Albany in 1900. B&A remained a distinctive part of the Central and its equipment was lettered for B&A until the 1950s. B&A caboose 1151 is preserved at Chester, Massachusetts. *Brian Solomon*

Shown here in September 2007, this Reading Company Class NMn wooden-bodied caboose is preserved on Pennsylvania's Wanamaker, Kempton & Southern Railroad. *Brian Solomon*

Reading Company Class NMn 62936 rolls across a grade crossing near Kempton, Pennsylvania. Today tourist railways such as the Wanamaker, Kempton & Southern offer visitors the opportunity to experience historic cabooses. *Brian Solomon*

Although some railroads opted for steel-body cabooses, Reading Company was among the lines that continued to order wooden-bodied cars into the 1940s. No. 62936 was built in September 1942. *Brian Solomon*

In its later service years, this former CV wooden-bodied van was operated by Vermont's Green Mountain Railroad as No. 41. In 2009 it was undergoing cosmetic restoration at Shelburne Falls. *Brian Solomon*

Privately owned and restored, CV No. 4014 passes Creamery Crossing on the Mass-Central on September 29, 1991. This 1925-built caboose is now preserved at the Railroad Museum of New England in Connecticut's Naugatuck Valley. *Brian Solomon*

This view shows the interior of a former Central Vermont "van," as CV's cabooses were known (the parlance taken from parent company Canadian National). CV's wooden-body cabooses were replaced in 1972 with modern steel extended-vision cars. Today this historic car is displayed at Shelburne Falls, Massachusetts. *Brian Solomon*

Above: In this March 3, 1957, view at Vergennes, Vermont, an Alco road switcher, a 40-foot company boxcar, and an antique wooden caboose symbolize the sad state of the Vermont-based Rutland Railway (historically the Rutland Railroad until reorganization in 1950). Declining traffic, increased highway competition, and restrictive labor arrangements doomed the line. Although it suspended operations in 1961, some of its lines were later reincarnated under the Vermont Railway and the Green Mountain Railroad. *Jim Shaughnessy*

Opposite bottom: On September 20, 1951, a pair of Rutland cabooses carry railway enthusiasts on a Chatham Exchange Club "Gay Nineties" excursion from Chatham, New York, to Rutland, Vermont, by way of the railroad's Corkscrew Division, as its Chatham Branch was known. This fabled stretch was abandoned in 1953, leaving little more than earthen embankments, memories, and a few prized photographs. *Jim Shaughnessy*

In June 1961, at Florence, Vermont, Rutland conductor Robert Thruston climbs aboard caboose No. 43 on a northbound local for Alburgh, Vermont. Rutland's wooden cabooses were similar to those of New York Central, which maintained a controlling interest in the Vermont line from 1904 to 1941. Rutland connected with the Central at Chatham, New York. *Jim Shaughnessy*

Delaware, Lackawanna & Western built this caboose at its Keyser Valley Shops in October 1948 using the frame from an old steam locomotive tender. Originally No. 885, DL&W preferred it for helper service because of its heavy frame. In 1976, Conrail inherited it from DL&W's successor, Erie Lackawanna, and later it was acquired by Genesee Valley Transportation. GVT renumbered it 4810 to reflect its build date and used it as shoving platform for reverse moves. Here, it is seen among the antiques at the Steamtown complex in Scranton, Pennsylvania, which was built on the site of the former DL&W shops. *Brian Solomon*

Until the 1980s, American short lines operated a variety of interesting cabooses. Arkansas & Louisiana Missouri Railway No. 484 is an unusually proportioned caboose photographed at Monroe, Louisiana, on August 14, 1985. Since 2004, the old A&LM has been operated by Genesee & Wyoming. *John Leopard*

Coal-hauling, three-foot-gauge East Broad Top ended common carrier operations in 1956. A scrapper bought the line and preserved most of the equipment, including some freight cars and cabooses. Since 1960, EBT has operated as a popular tourist line. On October 11, 1997, caboose 18 brings up the rear of an excursion rolling toward Rock Hill Furnace, Pennsylvania. *Brian Solomon*

Burlington Northern caboose No. 11444, seen at Seattle in August 1981, featured a stylish rounded cupola, perhaps the only one of its kind on BN. When BN was formed in 1970, the railroad had 1,060 cabooses, or "waycars," as they were known. *Thomas L. Carver*

BN inherited semi-streamlined, steel-body cabooses from one of its predecessor lines, Chicago, Burlington & Quincy. No. 10357, pictured at Lindenwood in St. Louis on November 23, 1984, was 1 of 30 such cars built for CB&Q in 1960. *Scott Muskopf*

Operator Bud Emmons hoops orders up to the conductor riding on BN caboose 10366 passing UP Junction at Tacoma, Washington, in the summer of 1978. CB&Q's semi-streamlined cabooses were a favorite of many observers. *Thomas L. Carver*

Five Union Pacific International Car Company center-cupola cabooses roll west on UP's busy Nebraska main line near Grand Island in September 1989. These cars were unusually tall, measuring 16 feet 1 1/4 inches from rail head to the top of the cupola. Similar cabooses built for the Norfolk & Western were only 14 feet 6 1/4 inches tall. *Brian Solomon*

UP cabooses ran through to Chicago over Chicago & North Western's main line, which forwarded the bulk of UP's transcontinental freight east of the Omaha/Council Bluffs gateway. On February 18, 1980, a UP center-cupola car on the back of a piggyback train passes a freight led by C&NW 870 at Sterling, Illinois. *John Leopard*

In a scene captured a few months before the similar photo on the preceding spread, Burlington Northern's Bud Emmons hoops orders to the UP local freight passing UP Junction at Tacoma, Washington. Improved communications, combined with widespread application of Centralized Traffic Control and better airbrake systems, made train orders and cabooses unnecessary. *Thomas L. Carver*

Alaska Railroad caboose 1078 rolling north passes a southward freight led by GP30 No. 2504 at Healy, Alaska, on August 30, 1985. *Thomas L. Carver*

Alaska Railroad's eclectic consists and spectacular scenery make for interesting images. At Girdwood on September 5, 1985, caboose 1077 seems incongruous with the mix of secondhand streamlined passenger cars assigned to ARR's Whittier Shuttle. *Thomas L. Carver*

ARR caboose 1077 rolls across a Pratt-style deck truss at Portage on September 5, 1985. The narrow angled cupola on a riveted-steel body was a design distinctive to ARR. *Thomas L. Carver*

Santa Fe 999470 at the back of freight 1-543-21 rolls west of Emporia, Kansas, on June 22, 1985. Santa Fe's typical late-era, steel-bodied, end-cupola cabooses were built by International Car Company and were 41 feet 9 inches long over coupler faces. The top of the cupola was just over 15 feet 6 inches above the rail. *Scott Muskopf*

The caboose on Santa Fe's 1-513-11 catches the setting sun on May 11, 1986. Cars such as this were equipped with 18-inch, shock-control underframes to minimize the effects of slack actions on crews. *Scott Muskopf*

At Southern Pacific's famed loop at Walong in California's Tehachapi Mountains, it was possible to frame both the head-end and tail-end of a long freight in the same photo. On September 24, 1983, a Santa Fe intermodal train works railroad timetable west at Walong with caboose 999591 at the back. Santa Fe had trackage rights on SP between Mojave and Kern Junction in Bakersfield. *Thomas L. Carver*

Above: In its final years, Nickel Plate Road (reporting marks NKP) bought some commercially manufactured bay-window cabooses that featured metal classification flags at the back. Car 425 was nearly new in this view. NKP was absorbed by Norfolk & Western in 1964. Today many of its main lines serve as important freight arteries for Norfolk Southern. *Jay Williams collection*

Opposite bottom: In the 1950s when New York Central diesels ground along the Water Level Route with mile-long freights, the NKP sprinted past on parallel tracks. Here an NKP conductor hails his competition. *J. William Vigrass*

NKP wooden off-center cupola caboose 263 was photographed at St. Marys, Ohio, on January 6, 1933. The Nickel Plate was among railroads that operated cabooses featuring fixed marker lamps on the cupola. *C. E. Helms photo, Jay Williams collection*

In March 1989, Norfolk Southern train 272 carries double-stacked Maersk containers for Canada below the old Buffalo Central Terminal. Efforts to improve productivity in the mid-1980s reduced crew sizes, implemented caboose-less freights, and introduced double-stacked container trains. As a result, photographs of cabooses at the back of double-stack trains are relatively rare. *Brian Solomon*

This old Norfolk & Western caboose was assigned to a local freight navigating trackage in downtown Roanoke, Virginia, on October 4, 2005. When built by International Car Company, it included crew bunks, lockers, toilet, sink, refrigerator, and hot plate—equipment necessary for long journeys. *Brian Solomon*

On April 9, 1988, the Norfolk Southern's "Wabash" rolls eastward on the old Nickel Plate Road main line west of Dunkirk, New York, with an N&W-era International Car Company center-cupola caboose at the back. The train, which crossed the International Bridge between Black Rock in Buffalo and Fort Erie, Ontario, still carried a caboose to comply with Canadian regulations.
Brian Solomon

In the 1980s, Canadian National "vans" were routinely operated on Central Vermont Railway freights south of St. Albans, Vermont. On March 3, 1987, CN 78117 is at the back of a local freight at Palmer, Massachusetts, carrying a brand-new Bombardier-built NJ Transit commuter car for interchange with Conrail. *Brian Solomon*

On July 4, 1987, Grand Trunk Western GP38 No. 5808 works the interchange track in Palmer, Massachusetts. Having made its drop at Conrail's Palmer Yard, the locomotive will couple onto CN caboose 78128, which came down on the through freight from St. Albans. Built in large numbers in the 1970s, CN's modern cabooses were 43 feet 4 1/2 inches long over coupler faces. *Brian Solomon*

Central Vermont's local freight 562 rolls northward with a CN van at Hospital Road in Monson, Massachusetts, on July 20, 1986. This was one of 30 CN vans (78100–78129) modified for international service during 1982 and 1983. The fixed semaphore is a distant signal for the Palmer diamond—the level crossing with Conrail's Boston Line (former Boston & Albany). *Brian Solomon*

Adirondack Scenic Railroad general manager Thomas L. Carver reviews his paperwork aboard a privately restored former Canadian National van operating on special excursions at Tupper Lake, New York, in October 2005. Large windows on these late-era cabooses provided crews a good view of their train. *Brian Solomon*

View from former CN caboose on the Adirondack Scenic Railroad at Tupper Lake, New York. *Brian Solomon*

A Canadian National 73100-series international service steel caboose brings up the back of Central Vermont freight 444 rolling across the Millers River at Millers Falls, Massachusetts, on July 13, 1988. CV's through freights were among the last road freights in New England regularly assigned manned cabooses. *Brian Solomon*

Above: Cape Breton & Central Nova Scotia is a Canadian National spinoff that operates former CN lines between Truro and Sydney, Nova Scotia, along with a couple of short branches. Although its road freights are caboose-less, the railroad had three former CN cabooses for local work. *Brian Solomon*

Opposite top: CB&CNS RS-18 No. 3852 and caboose 1000 are in the yard as the road freight from Sydney passes Stellarton on the evening of July 24, 1997. This caboose, named *The Enterprise*, was acquired secondhand from Canadian National, which in 1970 built its 472000-series vans from old boxcars. *Brian Solomon*

Opposite bottom: CB&CNS No. 1000 is former CN 78107 and among the railroad's vans cleared for international service. In 1980, Canadian railroads maintained an estimated 2,000 cabooses. However, a change in work rules in 1990 greatly reduced the need for cabooses. Most were subsequently sold or scrapped. *Brian Solomon*

New York, New Haven & Hartford—better known as "the New Haven"—was a pioneer in railroad intermodal operations. In July 1957, a Boston–to–New York City freight carrying piggyback trailers crosses the bridge at Cos Cob, Connecticut. At the back is C-589, a Class NE-5 caboose built by Pullman-Standard. Both the New Haven and Boston & Maine operated this style of car. *Jim Shaughnessy*

Above: At the back of a Penn Central freight at Harrison, New York, former New Haven C-573 rolls west on former home rails in March 1970, the year after the New Haven was absorbed by Penn Central. This World War II–era steel caboose still had a few years left in it. PC later rebuilt some as bay-window cabooses. *George W. Kowanski*

Left: Although B&M's Pullman-Standard cabooses were delivered in red paint, during the 1960s they were painted in B&M's new sky-blue livery. Here, B&M 443 catches the sun at Lawrence, Massachusetts, in August 1987. The ribbed steel-panel siding was characteristic of this type of car. *Brian Solomon*

Conrail's inherited N5c cabooses were already more than 30 years old when Conrail was formed in 1976, yet many served well into their fourth decade of service. On October 9, 1978, the conductor of an eastward Conrail freight grabs orders from an operator at Collinsville, Illinois. *Scott Muskopf*

The Pennsylvania Railroad built its N5c cabooses—which it referred to as "cabins"—during World War II. These became one of the most distinctive mass-produced, steel-body cabooses. PRR N5c No. 477926, built in April 1942, is seen here at Bradford, Ohio, in the early 1950s. The piping on the roof was for PRR's train phone—a pioneering application of railroad radio. *C. E. Helms photo, Jay Williams collection*

On August 11, 1987, the conductor on Conrail's NHSE (Cedar Hill Yard near New Haven, Connecticut, to Selkirk Yard, near Albany, New York) enjoys the morning sun from the back platform of an old Pennsylvania Railroad Class N5c at Springfield, Massachusetts. *Brian Solomon*

Pennsylvania Railroad N5c 477852 is preserved and displayed in Tuscan red paint near the west portals of the summit tunnels at Gallitzin, Pennsylvania. Built June 1942, it retains its classic porthole windows. *Brian Solomon*

After more than 40 years in service on PRR, Penn Central, and Conrail, this caboose recalls the tens of thousands of freights that passed through Gallitzin over the years. Today the vast majority of freights on the old PRR main line are caboose-less. *Brian Solomon*

The N5c is distinctive for its semi-streamlined design with porthole windows. It also carries visual cues borrowed from PRR's motive power of the same period. *Brian Solomon*

Another preserved Pennsylvania Railroad N5c is displayed at Emporium, Pennsylvania, near the former PRR main line from Harrisburg to Buffalo. *Brian Solomon*

The N5c's distinctive porthole windows on its sides and ends have long been a favorite design element of modelers and photographers. It was one of the most unusual caboose designs of its era. *Brian Solomon*

In the 1980s and 1990s railroads sold hundreds of cabooses to individuals and communities. Many line-side towns use these retired cars to display their railroad heritage and pay respect to the role that freight railroading played in American commerce. *Brian Solomom*

Erie Lackawanna wasn't winning many friends on this spring day in 1969. One of its long freights has blocked traffic in the streets of a small town on its line between Hoboken, New Jersey, and Binghamton, New York. Caboose C-260 has just cleared the crossing. The poster on the dash of the bus advertises a "Holiday Hippodrome Original Stage Circus," perhaps providing a clue as to the location of this photograph. *Richard Jay Solomon*

Above: An Erie Lackawanna work train makes a reverse move at Greycourt, New York, as the crew hangs onto caboose C864 in July 1975. In its later years, EL reversed its locomotive paint scheme for its caboose livery and the result was hailed as one of the most attractive ever applied to a caboose by a major railroad. *George W. Kowanski*

Opposite: On September 15, 1973, a pair of SD45s—including EL No. 801, originally an EMD demonstrator—provides 7,200 horsepower on the back of an eastward Central Railroad of New Jersey Hi Bridge Pool departing Scranton, Pennsylvania. This would have been a lot of power shoving on EL caboose C903, so the locomotives work ahead of the buggy. *George S. Pitarys*

Vermont's crew requirements allowed cabooses to survive on the Conn River Line several years after they had been largely discontinued from other Boston & Maine routes. On November 30, 1986, B&M 460 follows on the back of B&M's EDWJ (East Deerfield, Massachusetts, to White River Junction, Vermont) a few miles north of downtown Greenfield, Massachusetts. *Brian Solomon*

B&M 460 was a regular on Conn River freights in the mid-1980s. In August 1986 it rolls along the Connecticut River backwater at Vernon, Vermont. International Car Company built this class of cabooses in 1959 using frames from B&M wooden-bodied cars originally constructed in the 1920s by New Hampshire's Laconia Car Company. *Brian Solomon*

At 4:30 p.m. on August 14, 1987, a B&M local freight led by GP7 No. 1568 with caboose 460 at the back works through Greenfield, Massachusetts, toward the yards at East Deerfield. In the 1970s, the Federal Railroad Administration imposed a 40-year limit on cars interchanged between railroads. Since these cabooses had 1920s-era frames, they were limited to service on B&M routes and not permitted off line. *Brian Solomon*

On August 20, 1965, Lehigh Valley switcher 255 and Northeast-type caboose 95104 roll toward the station at Sayre, Pennsylvania. Sayre was the location of important classification yards and Lehigh Valley's primary locomotive shops. Although LV was melded into Conrail in 1976, the caboose picured on the opposite page is preserved near LV's 1881-built station that's now home to the Sayre Historical Society Museum. *Jim Shaughnessy*

In February 2010, Lehigh Valley 95011 basks in the sun compass west of the old Lehigh Valley yard in Sayre, where it passed through countless times during a career that spanned more than four decades. Today the old caboose provides a reminder of better days in the old shop town. *Brian Solomon*

Above: Lehigh Valley Northeast-type caboose 95003 is preserved at Steamtown in Scranton, Pennsylvania. *Brian Solomon*

Opposite top: Lehigh Valley A95068 is westbound at East Allentown, Pennsylvania, in February 1975. Note that the red paint is more akin to PRR's Tuscan red than the bright red often featured on cabooses. *George W. Kowanski*

Opposite bottom: Conrail Class N5b No. 18629 had seen better days, but was still very much active at the time of this March 28, 1986, photo taken in Hartford, Connecticut. *Brian Solomon*

Above: Reading Company Class NMj No. 92830 is preserved at the Wanamaker, Kempton & Southern, a tourist line connecting its namesake points on a former Reading branch line in eastern Pennsylvania. Reading and CNJ's operations were closely linked, which contributed to similarities in their cabooses. *Brian Solomon*

Opposite top: Bright-red Reading Company Northeast-style Class NMo caboose No. 94042 rolls through Cranford on Central Railroad of New Jersey's four-track main line prior to the Conrail takeover in April 1976. Built in August 1942, this caboose was typical of those operated by the railroad in later years. *Rich Zmijewski*

Opposite bottom: CNJ Class NE No. 91513 retains its traditional catwalks, as does the 40-foot boxcar to which it is coupled. Historically, brakemen were required to walk the tops of cars to set and release brakes. Although airbrakes obviated the need for this hazardous practice, brakemen walked the cars until the 1950s. *Rich Zmijewski*

Above: On May 23, 1990, through freight ROGJ-M (Roper Yard, Salt Lake City, Utah, to Grand Junction, Colorado) stalled west of Castilla, Utah, and the local nicknamed "the Midvale Tramp" was summoned to assist. After dropping their train, the local's trio of GP-30s tied onto the rear of unoccupied Rio Grande caboose 01431 and pushed them to Soldier Summit. The caboose was acting as a spacer between the pusher engines and the hazardous-material car ahead and therefore was unoccupied during the shove. *George S. Pitarys*

Opposite top: Denver & Rio Grande Western narrow gauge caboose 0574 trails a K36 Mikado working as a pusher on an eastward freight climbing toward Cumbres Pass near the New Mexico–Colorado state line on August 27, 1963. *Jim Shaughnessy*

Opposite bottom: Rio Grande Southern caboose 461 rides the back of a freight negotiating the famous Ophir Loop in southwestern Colorado. *The Sirman collection*

Above: A Cartier work extra rolls northward at milepost 30 immediately north of the Mac Donald Tunnel. The Cartier is an isolated ore conveyor that runs from the mine at Mont Wright to Port Cartier, Quebec, traversing large tracts of wilderness inhabited only by moose, deer, and thick swarms of vicious, man-eating flies. *Brian Solomon*

Opposite top: Le Nord Côtier is one of four cabooses built for Cartier by Morrison in 1960. *Brian Solomon*

Opposite bottom: Cartier caboose *Le Nord Côtier* works north with a work train at milepost 42.8 in Quebec's Sept-Îles National Park. Much of the landscape penetrated by this railway is inaccessible by road. *Brian Solomon*

Chapter 2

Bay-Windows

Bay-Windows

The cupola design posed difficulties. The high, elevated perch was a dangerous place to ride; an accident or heavy slack action might send a crewman tumbling to the floor. The cupola also tended to draw heat from the whole car. And as freight cars grew, the height required to see over them increased. This was especially problematic for lines with restrictive overhead clearances.

Railroads developed an alternative to the cupola in the form of side-mounted bay windows. This design change was not universally accepted, but coincided with the general shift from wooden-bodied designs to all-steel construction. As a result, most bay-window cars had steel bodies.

While side-mounted bay windows had been used on some railroad equipment as early as the 1850s, application of the bay window was not common until the twentieth century. Historian John H. White Jr. notes in his book, *The American Railroad Freight Car*, that the bay-window caboose was introduced in its modern form by the Akron, Canton & Youngstown railroad in 1923.

Baltimore & Ohio, however, was the true bay-window pioneer. In 1931, B&O constructed a single, all-steel bay-window caboose. This prototype, No. 2500, offered greater floor space than comparable cupola cabooses. B&O also felt this arrangement offered a better lateral view of a freight train than did cupola designs. When B&O experimented with this all-steel prototype, it had a fleet of roughly 1,200 wooden-bodied cupola cabooses in service. This fleet, combined with declining freight traffic in the Great Depression, delayed mass-production of bay-window designs. In 1936, B&O finally moved toward bay-window construction, first introducing two additional prototypes: all-steel cars with distinctive wraparound bracing and known as "wagon-top" designs because of their conceptual similarity to the old horsedrawn Conestoga wagons. During World War II, when freight traffic increased rapidly, B&O adopted a more Spartan style of bay-window caboose. This featured a wooden body to accommodate wartime steel shortages, but was built on a steel frame and had steel observatories.

Another early bay-window proponent was Milwaukee Road, which adopted the design in 1939. By eliminating the cupola, Milwaukee found it could provide more spacious accommodation for its crews. Milwaukee Road had long built much of its own equipment and at the end of World War II initiated an intensive caboose rebuilding program, producing approximately 900 cabooses. The body used Milwaukee's distinctive horizontal ribbed sheathing previously used on its *Hiawatha* passenger cars and other rolling stock. Milwaukee removed cupolas and interior partitions from older cars while installing bay windows, modern cook stoves, lockers, sinks, and toilets with running water.

New York Central was another large user of early bay-window designs. Central's historic Water Level Route from New York to Chicago has some of the most restrictive vertical clearances on any main line in the United States. After World War II, the railroad acquired hundreds of steel-bodied cars to replace older wooden-body cupola cabooses. Its new cars featured a distinctive partial bay that offered the optimum position

a railroader would need to lean into the window, but required just a small amount of steel to produce.

In the mid-1950s, Southern Pacific and Western Pacific were among the roads that favored bay-windows in the West, while in the South, Southern Railway ordered hundreds of the type. In the Midwest, Chicago & North Western and Nickel Plate Road embraced bay-windows. As demand grew, commercial manufacturers stepped in to offer standardized bay-window cars. Among the most common commercially designed cars were those built by International Car Company. A typical International Car bay-window caboose measured 36 feet 7 1/4 inches long over the end plates, 11 feet 10 3/8 inches tall, and 8 feet 7 3/8 inches wide with each bay window protruding roughly 1 foot from the side of the car. The caboose weighed between 65,000 and 70,000 pounds depending on buyer options, and the sides were made of flat steel while the roof was corrugated. Fruit Growers Express also built bay-window cabooses to a similar pattern.

Previous pages:
A Penn Central freight works east on the Boston & Albany at Chatham, New York. At the back is a former New York Central bay-window caboose still lettered with New York Central's obsolete (and, in this context, ironic) "Road to the Future" slogan. Three years earlier the Central merged with the Pennsylvania Railroad to form Penn Central, which soon descended into bankruptcy.
George W. Kowanski

Above: At 10:52 a.m. on November 14, 1948, Baltimore & Ohio C2447 bears the brunt of Mallet compounds 7046 and 7039 working as pushers on an eastward coal train near the top of the Cranberry Grade at Terra Alta, West Virginia. *Bruce D. Fales photo, Jay Williams collection*

Opposite top: At 4 p.m. on July 9, 1958, B&O wagon-top cabooses are being refurbished at Glenwood Shops in Pittsburgh. The steel-body, bay-window, wagon-top caboose was a uniquely B&O creation. Between 1941 and 1945, its Keyser, West Virginia, shops turned out 125 of the cars, originally B&O Class I-12. The cars measured 32 feet 5 inches long. *Richard Jay Solomon*

Opposite bottom: In the 1980s, operational changes and smaller crews resulted in caboose-less freights as well as a caboose surplus. A long line of old Baltimore & Ohio cabooses sits at the railroad's Cumberland, Maryland, yard in May 1985. Included are some of B&O's venerable wagon tops dating from World War II. *Brian Solomon*

Above: In February 1976, Baltimore & Ohio bay-window C-2895 makes for a good contrast with Central Railroad of New Jersey Northeast-style cupola cabooses at Elizabethport, New Jersey. The Northeast design was popular with anthracite railroads, while in the later-era B&O preferred bay-window designs. The B&O caboose, classified by Chessie System as a C-23, was a standard type on the railroad and was built at various company shops between 1953 and 1965. *George W. Kowanski.*

Opposite top: On July 27, 1987, a Chessie System bay-window is assigned to a work train on the west slope of Baltimore & Ohio's Sand Patch Grade in southwestern Pennsylvania. Chessie System Class C-26A No. 903830 was one of 97 standard bay-window cabooses built for B&O by International Car Company in 1975. *Brian Solomon*

Opposite bottom: Chesapeake & Ohio 904115 in classic Chessie System paint sits in the old B&O yard at Johnstown, Pennsylvania, on February 8, 1990. Built by Fruit Growers Express in 1980, it was part of the final order of Chessie System cabooses. The Staggers Act of 1980 helped deregulate American railroads and accelerated the move toward caboose-less freights as railroads sought to improve labor productivity. *Patrick Yough*

Above: Baltimore & Ohio bay-window C-2884 was restored in blue and yellow paint for display at the Baltimore & Ohio Railroad Museum in Baltimore. B&O's Class I-17A caboose was produced at a variety of company shops over a 12-year span beginning in 1953. A relatively short, steel-bodied caboose, it measured 30 feet over end sills and was just more than 34 feet 8 inches over coupler faces. *Tom Kline.*

Opposite top: At 4 p.m. on July 24, 1958, westward B&O freight 91 with C-2301 on its tail end waits as eastward 98, led by a pair of Electro-Motive F-units, passes at Sandoval, Illinois, on the B&O route to St. Louis. B&O built 175 Class I-16 cabooses from old boxcars during the wartime traffic surge in 1942 and 1943. Many served for three or more decades. *Richard Jay Solomon*

Opposite bottom: CSX's Detroit-to-Buffalo turn passes a Conrail piggyback train in Buffalo in March 1989. By this time most through freights in the United States were caboose-less, but since the CSX train used the old Pere Marquette route via Ontario and Niagara Falls, it continued to carry a caboose to meet Canadian requirements. CSX 904156 was only nine years old in this photograph. *Brian Solomon*

A Missouri Pacific bay-window brings up the tail of a 13-car freight led by Union Pacific's Alco-built 4-8-4 No. 844. The train is working its way west on UP's double-track transcontinental line across Nebraska in September 1989. Although steam locomotive 844 was normally reserved for excursion service, on this day it had a rare opportunity to haul freight. *Brian Solomon*

On June 14, 1987, several years after the so-called "Mop-Up" merger, Missouri Pacific bay-window caboose 13837 punctuates an eastward UP freight north of Eureka, Missouri. *Scott Muskopf*

Seen here in August 2009, Missouri Pacific 13878 is one of several cabooses preserved at the Western Pacific Railroad Museum in Portola, California.
Brian Solomon

Above: A conductor riding in Erie Lackawanna bay-window caboose C307 gazes forward. Notice the large "wagon-wheel" radio antenna atop the center of the caboose. EL was an early user of train radio—technology that ultimately contributed to the demise of the caboose. *Rich Zmijewski*

Opposite top: In this classic scene from July 1964, an Erie Lackawanna bay-window caboose marks the end of a long mixed freight carrying everything from traditional oil tank cars and 40-foot boxcars, to modern TOFC (trailer-on-flatcar) piggyback trailers. *Richard Jay Solomon*

Opposite bottom: Like many American railroads, Erie Lackawanna painted equipment for the nation's Bicentennial. Caboose C354 displays its resplendent patriotic livery at Croxton Yard near Secaucus, New Jersey. By July 4, 1976, Erie Lackawanna was melded into the new Conrail system. *Rich Zmijewski*

Above: Missouri-Kansas-Texas Railroad—better known as "The Katy"—connected the St. Louis and Kansas City with Ft. Worth, Dallas, San Antonio, and Houston, Texas. Resting at the yard in Kansas City, Kansas, on April 23, 1981, MKT 60 was a heavy, homebuilt, bay-window caboose. *Scott Muskopf*

Opposite top: Sacramento Northern 1642 was a rare example of a wooden-bodied, bay-window caboose converted from an old freight car. Although markings on the side of the car indicate it was built in October 1916, the steel bay-window was certainly a later addition. On July 3, 1976, it was seen on Western Pacific's San Francisco terminal trackage south of Market Street on Berry Street. *Brian Jennison*

Opposite bottom: During World War II, Kansas City Southern shop forces created their own cabooses by converting old 40-foot wood-and-steel boxcars into awkwardly proportioned bay-window cabooses such as this number 385. After the war the railroad bought standard styles offered by manufacturers but continued to use these "economy" cars into the mid-1980s. In their later days these cars were used mainly in local, maintenance-of-way, and switching service. In July 1984, No. 385, with its classic porthole windows, lays over outside the depot at Sulphur Springs, Texas, on KCS's Tidewater turn, a local job that handles coal trains from a nearby mine to an area power plant. *Lewis Raby, Tom Kline collection*

Built by International Car, Southern Pacific Class C-40-6 No. 1779 brings up the rear of through freight MERV-M (Medford, Oregon, to Roseville, California) while working toward Siskiyou Summit on the 3 percent grade near old Foliage, Oregon. *Brian Solomon*

Southern Pacific's Grants Pass turn works past Union Switch & Signal lower-quadrant semaphores in Oregon's Rogue River Valley on May 4, 1990. The classic steel-bodied, bay-window caboose makes a silhouette against irrigation spray in the afternoon sun. *Brian Solomon*

In the early 1990s, SP's Siskiyou Line local freights, as well as Siskiyou road freights, continued to use cabooses. Having ascended the most difficult mainline grade on the Siskiyou Line, SP's freight MERV-M disappears into the west portal of the Siskiyou Summit Tunnel in May 1990. *Brian Solomon*

In May 1990, a Southern Pacific Class C-40-7 bay-window punctuates a local freight working past milepost 454 on the 5.8-mile White City Branch that diverges from SP's Siskiyou Line at Tolo, Oregon. The dormant volcanic cone of Mount McLoughlin looms in the distance. *Brian Solomon*

The bucolic scenery of Oregon's Rogue River Valley, combined with antique railroad signals and freights with cabooses, made the Siskiyou Line an interesting locale in the early 1990s. SP's tri-weekly EUME-M (Eugene to Medford, Oregon) hauls bay-window No. 1938, a Class C-50-5 built by International Car in 1974. *Brian Solomon*

SP SD9 No. 4344 shoves a work train across the Wall Creek Trestle toward Siskiyou Summit on May 11, 1990. By 1990, the Siskiyou Line was among the last routes on SP where cabooses were routinely operated. Yet, work trains across the SP continued to require cabooses for some years to come. *Brian Solomon*

Above: Southern Pacific's MERV-M ascends the 3 percent grade between Ashland and Siskiyou Summit in April 1990. The caboose is passing a set of 1910-vintage Union Switch & Signal lower-quadrant semaphores. To the right of the signals is the flasher light for the defect detector. In the event of a train defect the light would flash, alerting the crew on the caboose. *Brian Solomon*

Opposite top: Passing the old timetable station at Gazelle, California, SP's MERV-M (Medford, Oregon, to Roseville, California) rolls toward Black Butte, California, where the Siskiyou Line joins the Cascade Route. Mount Shasta looms majestically above the train. *Brian Solomon*

Opposite bottom: Most SP cabooses were painted in traditional rust brown with white lettering, which matched the railroad's boxcars and other freight equipment. In May 1990, SP's RVME-M (Roseville, California, to Medford, Oregon) rolls through the barren confines of Ager Canyon near the California–Oregon border. Cotton Belt was an SP affiliate operating lines in east Texas, Louisiana, Arkansas, and Missouri. *Brian Solomon*

Above: Southern Pacific's unique "shorty" bay-window prototype is propelled downgrade with the water train by a pair of SD9s at Long Ravine, California, during summer 1990. A Loram rail-grinding train was working the line, raising the risk of fire. *Brian Solomon*

Opposite top: In 1980, SP built a short bay-window prototype that the railroad classed C-50-10, numbered SP-1, and painted in its famous *Daylight* colors. Here the caboose is at the end of an SP work train shoving westward on the No. 1 track west of New Castle, California, on February 10, 1990. *Brian Solomon*

Opposite bottom: To minimize fire risk in the dry summer heat of the Sierra, SP historically operated water trains on its Donner Pass crossing. Originally water trains were needed to protect dozens of miles of snowsheds. In modern times they are primarily employed to combat brush fires. Here a water train with caboose SP-1 is in the siding at Gold Run, California, as an eastward SP freight ascends the Sierra. *Brian Solomon*

At Thousand Palms, California, in February 1990, an eastward Southern Pacific stack train is viewed from the back platform of caboose 4708. *Brian Solomon*

Spartan bay-window cabooses and utilitarian Union Switch & Signal searchlights typified SP's modern image as a freight hauler. In February 1990, a work train holds the siding at Thousand Palms, California, as it waits for a procession of eastward intermodal trains. Bay-window No. 4708 was one of 75 Class C-50-9 cabooses that were among the last built for SP. *Brian Solomon*

Above: Caboose 10958 was typical of Chicago & North Western's later years. On April 19, 1995, the conductor of the Jefferson Junction local rides the rear platform as his train makes a reverse move around the wye at the junction in preparation for its evening run up to Clyman Junction. In a few weeks time the old C&NW was formally folded into the Union Pacific. *Brian Solomon*

Opposite top: C&NW's International Car caboose 10958 rolls along near Johnson Creek, Wisconsin. The Jefferson Junction local made a weekday roundtrip from its Wisconsin namesake to Clyman Junction and was one of the last C&NW freights to regularly warrant a caboose. *Brian Solomon*

Opposite bottom: A trainload of former C&NW bay-window cabooses heads for the scrapyard aboard TTX flats. *Scott Muskopf*

Above: Although Milwaukee Road was among the pioneers of the bay-window caboose, initially using homebuilt designs, in later years it purchased commercially built bay-windows such as this one working a Soo Line local freight at Madison, Wisconsin, on August 4, 1987. *Scott Muskopf*

Opposite top: Milwaukee Road was among the earliest large railroads to adopt the bay-window design. Its first bay-windows were built by its Milwaukee, Wisconsin, shops using ribbed-sided, steel-body construction. Typical was caboose 01885, photographed here at Sioux City, Iowa, on May 16, 1948. *Jay Williams collection*

Opposite bottom: Milwaukee Road caboose 992177 is seen at Madison, Wisconsin, in July 1987. By the 1980s the glory days of the caboose were long gone and many surviving examples were battle-worn veterans with decades of hard service behind them. *Scott Muskopf*

Union Pacific was famous for painting slogans on its cabooses. This one on former Western Pacific bay-window 24515 reads "What do we do? We work for you" and is attributed to Henry C. Fricke of Denver, Colorado. *Brian Solomon*

On February 23, 1992, a UP bomb train, complete with a former Western Pacific bay-window caboose, rolls east along the old Sacramento Northern near Pittsburg, California. The Sacramento Northern system was under control of the WP for many years, serving as a feeder. WP was acquired by Union Pacific in 1981. *Brian Solomon*

A fragment of the old Sacramento Northern interurban network survived until the mid-1990s to serve the Concord Naval Weapons Station near Concord, California. Former WP caboose 24515 brings up the tail of a short "bomb train" in the cut where the line crossed beneath Santa Fe's line to Richmond, California. *Brian Solomon*

Above: Union Pacific and Burlington Northern shared trackage on the Oregon Trunk north of Bend to the Columbia River. On June 30, 1994, UP's tri-weekly Bend local freight rolls northward past a BN work train at Gateway, Oregon. In the mid-1990s, nearly a decade after they had been largely discontinued on other lines, cabooses were still the rule on the "OT." *Brian Solomon*

Opposite top: On the longest days of the year in the Pacific Northwest, light holds in the sky until after 10 p.m. As dusk fades on June 30, 1994, UP's Bend local on the Oregon Trunk rolls northward across a steel trestle. *Brian Solomon*

Opposite bottom: On February 15, 1981, Union Pacific 25819 passes Rock Island's Short Line Junction tower near Des Moines, Iowa. This caboose was built in 1979 by International Car Company, which described the car style as a modified short-body bay-window. *John Leopard*

Conrail maintained New York Central's tradition of painting cabooses with safety slogans. This specially painted N-7 was the New England Division caboose, but by 1986 had been reassigned to Conrail's Buffalo Division where it regularly worked out of Goodman Street Yard in Rochester. *Brian Solomon*

At 5:23 p.m. on the afternoon of April 10, 1987, Conrail's Buffalo Division caboose pauses on the former New York Central main line east of Churchville, New York. Clean Conrail B36-7 No. 5054, leading westward Trail Van symbol freight TV-9 (Boston–Chicago trailers), blasts past local freight WBRO-15 working eastward along the Water Level Route from Batavia to Rochester. *Brian Solomon*

This view from the bay-window of specially painted Buffalo Division Class N7 caboose 21736 on April 10, 1987, looks east on Conrail's former New York Central Water Level Route near Chili Junction, New York. *Brian Solomon*

Above: A Conrail N21 caboose works the back of a local freight at West Springfield Yard, Massachusetts, on the morning of New Year's Eve 1988. *Brian Solomon*

Opposite top: Conrail Class N21 caboose 21262 is at the back of local freight WBRO-15 working Genesee Junction Yard on the old New York, West Shore & Buffalo line near Mortimer, New York in April 1987. *Brian Solomon*

Opposite bottom: In April 1988 two SW1500s make a reverse move on the former New York Central main line across the former Pennsylvania Railroad crossing at Erie, Pennsylvania. Aiding in the shove move is Class N21 caboose 21208. *Brian Solomon*

Above: Providence & Worcester bay-window 5001 rolls east out of the siding and past the closed former New Haven Railroad interlocking tower at Old Saybrook, Connecticut. *Brian Solomon*

Opposite top: P&W freights from Plainfield and New Haven routinely swapped cars along Amtrak's Northeast Corridor at Old Saybrook, Connecticut. In these December 6, 1993, views, P&W bay-window 5001 brings up the tail end of a freight of gravel cars heading eastward along the old New Haven Shore Line Route toward Groton. *Brian Solomon*

Opposite bottom: P&W bay-window caboose 5001 at Old Saybrook, Connecticut. *Brian Solomon*

Above: Former Frisco bay-window caboose 1734, renumbered as Burlington Northern 11709, brings up the back of a northbound empty grain train approaching the Hargrave Road crossing north of Houston, Texas, on February 2, 1981. Built by the Frisco shop forces in Springfield, Missouri, in December 1979, the nearly pristine appearance of this caboose is blemished only by the hastily applied number patch of its new owner. *Tom Kline*

Opposite top: The St. Louis–San Francisco Railway—commonly known as the Frisco—didn't make it any farther west or south than the Texas Panhandle until 1980 when it was absorbed by BN. On January 4, 1981, former Frisco 11703 rolls past the old Frisco station at Webster Groves, Missouri. The Frisco boasted 5,000 miles in 10 states from Missouri to Florida. *John Leopard*

Opposite bottom: Circus World Museum's bay-window caboose brings up the tail of the museum's popular circus train rolling west on the Wisconsin & Southern on July 8, 1996. The museum is located in Baraboo, Wisconsin. *Brian Solomon*

Above: Southern Railway X554 marks the end of a westward freight as viewed from the relative shelter offered by the back platform of an open-end observation car on an excursion train in southern Indiana on June 3, 1979. Today, Southern's once unremarked St. Louis line is a busy part of the NS empire. *Scott Muskopf*

Opposite top: On a clear January 23, 1985, Southern Railway eastbound 111 near Belleville, Illinois, carries ITEL containers on TTX flatcars with caboose X436 bringing up the rear. Many of Southern's late-era bay-windows were built by Gantt Manufacturing of South Carolina. *Scott Muskopf*

Opposite bottom: Southern Railway freight 112 at St. Louis, Missouri, carries classic bay-window caboose X398 on its way to Norfolk & Western's Luther Yard. Southern freights terminated at Coapman Yard in East St. Louis, Illinois, until Southern Railway came under Norfolk Southern control in 1982. More than 265 Southern Railway cabooses have been preserved in 24 states. *Scott Muskopf*

Above: On April 12, 1979, Louisville & Nashville GP7 No. 476 has taken the siding at Rentchler, Illinois, to let an East St. Louis–bound freight pass. Bringing up the rear is bay-window 6382, freshly painted in the livery of the Family Lines, a 1970s umbrella organization that combined L&N, Seaboard Coast Line, and affiliated properties. It was later consolidated as the Seaboard System, a component of modern-day CSX. *Scott Muskopf*

Opposite top: L&N bay window 6254 rides the tail end of a westward freight rolling through the snow near Belleville, Illinois, on January 25, 1979. CSX abandoned the tracks in the late 1980s, but they were rebuilt in 2001 as part of an extension of St. Louis' MetroLink light-rail transit system. *Scott Muskopf*

Opposite bottom: Clinchfield Railroad was among the lines operated by the Family Lines network. Clinchfield 1111 was a relatively short-frame bay-window caboose built by Fruit Growers Express at Alexandria, Virginia. On April 18, 1981, it was photographed at Erwin, Tennessee, in fresh Family Lines paint. *Photographer unknown, Tom Kline collection*

Above: Bessemer & Lake Erie's International Car bay-window 2001 catches the sun with a pair of SD9s at Calvin Yard in Butler, Pennsylvania, in January 1998. *Patrick Yough*

Opposite top: Union Railroad C-100 is a survivor. On September 22, 2007, this former B&LE caboose rolls slowly upgrade with a loaded coke train. *Brian Solomon*

Opposite bottom: Union Railroad C-1030 is an unusually short bay-window type. Here it is seen at the Union's yards at Duquesne, Pennsylvania, on September 26, 1987. *Gordon Lloyd Jr., photo, Patrick Yough collection*

Chapter 3

Wide-Vision

Wide-Vision

Traditionally cabooses were tailor-built to individual railroad plans either at railroad car shops or by commercial car builders. The railways' individual requirements resulted in great variations in design. Later some standardized caboose designs emerged, such as the Northeast type common to anthracite roads. In the postwar steel-car era, commercial car manufacturers began marketing cabooses of their own standard designs. Among these was the International Car Company of Buffalo, New York, which built cars at its Kenton, Ohio, plant, and later became a division of Paccar. By the 1960s it was one of the last independent commercial caboose manufacturers, and offered two standard all-steel types widely adopted by North American railroads. One of International Car's common late-era designs was the International Extra Wide Vision Caboose. This was considered a hybrid design that combined some benefits of both bay-window and cupola designs. International wasn't the first to adopt this type, as Midwestern carriers such as Chicago Great Western, Duluth, Missabe & Iron Range, and Wabash

had variously experimented with wide-vision cars. Ultimately, International Car was the greatest proponent of this style and the only commercial manufacturer in the United States to produce the design on a wide scale.

Among the extra–wide vision designs was a long-body car with large end platforms and a total length of 49 feet 3¼ inches over pulling faces, while the body was 9 feet 7 inches over sills, and the cupola was 10 feet 8 inches wide, rising 14 feet 8⅝ inches over rail level. Another wide-vision design was shorter, measuring just less than 42 feet between coupler faces with the body of the car between strikers measuring 39 feet 1½ inches. Some cars were equipped with Darby Corporation cushioned underframes, others with Waugh-cushioned underframes. Most were built with Barber Bettendorf swing-motion trucks, whose elliptical springs were designed for the constant load of a typical caboose in freight service. Unlike other freight equipment, cabooses were not designed to accept a heavy load and therefore had different truck requirements than load-bearing freight cars. In the modern era, roller bearings were required on new equipment, so the vast majority of late-era cabooses, including International's, were roller bearing–equipped, typically with Timken bearings.

In the late caboose era, the International extra–wide vision cars were among the most common types of new cupola cabooses used in the United States, operating from the coast of Maine to southern California and from the Cascades to the southern Appalachians. Although these were built to standard plans, some elements of the design varied from railroad to railroad, including window placement, and, of course, individual railroad livery.

These cabooses were favored by Burlington Northern, which had inherited many of the cars from its predecessor lines. As late as the mid-1990s, Burlington Northern routinely operated cabooses on several of its mainline routes, including the Oregon Trunk between Klamath Falls, Oregon, and the Columbia River at Wishram, Washington, and on the former Northern Pacific main line across North Dakota. On other large railroads extra–wide vision cars were relatively obscure. Conrail, for example, inherited just a handful from the Reading Company, and the type was rare on that line compared with the hordes of former New York Central bay-window cars and Pennsylvania Railroad steel-bodied cupola types.

Previous pages:
A Burlington Northern wide-vision caboose, with a modern-day telemetry device on its back coupler, brings up the tail end of a loaded Powder River coal train rolling eastward on the old Northern Pacific main line near Sully Springs, North Dakota, on July 14, 1994. *Brian Solomon*

An eastward Maine Central freight navigates New Hampshire's famed Crawford Notch with a modern extended-vision caboose in the railroad's yellow and green paint at the back. This line was closed to through freight traffic in 1983, but the most dramatic portions reopened as the Conway Scenic Railroad. *Jim Shaughnessy*

St. Maries River Railroad extended-vision caboose No. 994 sits quietly at the back of a timber train at St. Maries, Idaho, on July 4, 1994. Since 1980, this railroad operated on former Milwaukee Road trackage, handling freight business consisting largely of timber traffic originating in the Idaho panhandle. *Brian Solomon*

The Department of Defense maintains cabooses for monitoring its hazardous materials trains. On the morning of May 14, 1988, DODX 904—an International Car extended-vision caboose—brings up the rear of a Delaware & Hudson hazardous materials extra at Carsons near Canisteo, New York. *Brian Solomon*

D&H operated via trackage rights over Conrail on the former Erie Railroad between Binghamton and Buffalo, New York. Most of its trains were conventional freight or double-stacked containers, but on May 14, 1988, D&H had a special move: carrying heavy metals for the Department of Defense. In the early hours the train moves stealthily through fog in the Canisteo River Valley at Adrian, New York. Notice that the telemetry device on the rear coupler is active and lit. *Brian Solomon*

Later on the same morning, D&H's heavy-metal move, operating as EBBU (East Binghamton to Buffalo) approaches Dalton, New York. *Brian Solomon*

At 11:16 a.m. on November 16, 1993, a weather-worn Soo Line wide-vision caboose at the back of a freight rolls into the short tunnel at East Westminster in St. Paul, Minnesota. *Brian Solomon*

Canadian Pacific local G-41 rolls southward at 31st Street in Chicago on November 11, 2008, with an old Soo Line caboose at the back of double-stacks. Despite its obsolescence, the caboose survives in a few places. *Brian Solomon*

A westward Soo Line freight crosses the Mississippi River at Minneapolis. Soo Line continued to regularly assign cabooses to freights into the mid-1990s. *Brian Solomon*

January 13, 1994, was abnormally cold and it couldn't have been too cozy inside of this old Soo Line wide-vision caboose nearing Pig's Eye Yard in St. Paul, Minnesota. *Brian Solomon*

Above and opposite: A new cab-control car bound for San Diego area *Coaster* passenger service. *Coaster* makes for an interesting juxtaposition with the tatty Soo Line caboose trailing it on this southward CP Rail freight rolling along the banks of the Mississippi in Iowa on September 10, 1994. *Brian Solomon*

Three CP Rail cabooses roll west at Dorval, Quebec, with a COFC (container-on-flatcar) train in May 1985. The two rear cabooses (434540 built by Angus shops in 1975, and the trailing 434575 built in 1977) are the wide-vision type popular on Canadian Pacific in its later caboose-operating years. Many American railroads had begun to discontinue caboose operation by 1985, but CP Rail still assigned them to most through and local freight trains until 1990 when they began to be replaced by telemetry devices and modern work rules. *Brian Solomon*

At 1:34 p.m. on August 25, 1986, CP Rail 434951 rolls across the Pleasant River east of the yard at Brownville Junction, Maine. CP's late-era cabooses were painted mustard yellow with its famous "Pac-Man" logo prominently displayed on their sides. This caboose was one of eight center-cupola, steel cabooses built by CP's Angus shops in 1977 for international service. *Brian Solomon*

CP Rail 434538 is coated with ice from its duty in plow service at Ste. Thérèse, Quebec, on March 1, 1992. It was 1 of 31 steel, center-cupola types built at the Angus Shops in 1975. *Thomas L. Carver*

After a 1984 restructuring, the British Columbia Railway became known as BC Rail. Here, BC Rail extended-vision 1872, built at the Squamish Shops in 1973, rolls south on extra 718 near Fountain in August 1989. BC Rail was sold to Canadian National in 2003–2004. *Thomas L. Carver*

Sequentially numbered BC Rail cabooses meet at Tisdale on August 30, 1983. Both 1880 and 1881 were products of the railroad's Squamish Shops. The railroad's cabooses were relatively prosaic modern cars, but railway enthusiasts were attracted to the line for its Alco diesels and dramatic scenery. *Thomas L. Carver*

In time-honored tradition, the conductor aboard BC Rail 23 south is ready to grab orders from the operator at Pemberton. Caboose 1961 was nearly 20 years old at the time of this 1990 photograph. *Thomas L. Carver*

Above: New Santa Fe extended-vision caboose 999702, resplendent in red paint, rests at Bakersfield, California, on March 8, 1978. The caboose was less than two months old at the time of the photograph. *Grant Flanders photo, Brian Jennison collection*

Opposite top: A train of empty military flatcars is viewed from the cupola of a Santa Fe Class Ce-11 extended-vision caboose passing south through El Pleasant, Texas, on July 27, 1991. The heavy-duty flatcars are destined for a seaport on the Houston ship channel to load tanks and armored vehicles returning from the Persian Gulf War and then return them to Ft. Hood in central Texas. Built by International Car, Santa Fe's Ce-11 Class "waycars" were the newest, most modern cabooses in the fleet and sported such amenities as cupola windshield wipers and sunshades (partially drawn in this photo). *Tom Kline*

Opposite bottom: At Collier, California, on November 4, 1983, a short westward Santa Fe freight rolls toward Richmond, California, bathed in evening light diffused by Bay Area smog. *Brian Jennison*

Above: Central Vermont extra–wide vision caboose 4040 moves northward into the State Line siding between Stafford, Connecticut, and Monson, Massachusetts, on May 18, 1985. *Brian Solomon*

Opposite top: In August 1989, a summer shower has just cleared at Dublin Street in Palmer, Massachusetts, at the south end of the yard where Central Vermont caboose 4045, on the back of a local freight, rests alongside some of the railroad's venerable GP9s. *Brian Solomon*

Opposite bottom: In the 1980s, CV's Palmer Subdivision trains were characterized by first-generation Electro-Motive GP9s and 1972 vintage extended-vision cabooses. On December 27, 1987, train No. 444 has just arrived at Palmer from St. Albans, Vermont, behind a former Rock Island GP18, while caboose 4044 is at the back of local freight 562. *Brian Solomon*

Above: On the morning of October 8, 1991, Central Vermont Railway 444 has just cleared the junction at East Northfield on its final leg of its trip from St. Albans, Vermont, to Palmer, Massachusetts. At the back is extra–wide vision caboose 4044. Ahead of the caboose is a pair of Bombardier-built commuter cars for New York–area suburban train operator Metro-North that will be interchanged with Conrail at Palmer. *Brian Solomon*

Opposite top: Canadian National and Central Vermont cabooses rest between runs at the yard in Palmer, Massachusetts, on June 4, 1987. CN operated CV as a subsidiary until February 1995 when the operation was sold to RailTex and became known as New England Central. By that time caboose-less freights were standard on the line. *Brian Solomon*

Opposite bottom: In the early 1970s, the CV replaced wooden-bodied cabooses, such as 4030 pictured here, with new International Car extra–wide vision cars. *Vic Newton photo, Robert A. Buck collection*

Minutes from Lindenwood Yard in St. Louis, Frisco No. 36 glides through Webster Groves, Missouri, on August 9, 1980, with extended-vision caboose C1705 at the rear. Both the cupola windows and back door are wide open, suggesting the need for a steady draft on a hot, humid day. *Scott Muskopf*

Less than two months after the merger, Burlington Northern's influence on the former Frisco was already showing. BN train 370 rolls through Nichols Junction, Missouri, on January 17, 1981, with a pair of extended-vision cabooses. One will probably be dropped off at either Columbus or Fort Scott, Kansas, for local service. *Scott Muskopf*

Frisco caboose 1266 brings up the back of train 32 eastbound at Rolla, Missouri, on the morning of December 14, 1979. This was considered the hottest eastbound train on the railway, and along with westbound counterpart 33, carried trailers between Irving, Texas, and St. Louis. Cabooses on these trains were always in for a fast ride. *Scott Muskopf*

Above: Burlington Northern extended-vision caboose 10631 was still wearing Chicago, Burlington & Quincy paint when it was photographed in November 1977. This BN southbound is on Alton & Southern Railway tracks in Washington Park, Illinois. The CB&Q was among the lines that described their cabooses as waycars. *Scott Muskopf*

Opposite top: On August 18, 1981, an eastward BN freight passing East Dubuque carries a collection of modern steel cabooses. Notice the lower side windows have been blocked on several of the extended-vision cabooses. Many railroads covered up extra windows in later years to avoid vandalism and the need to install expensive safety glass. *John Leopard*

Opposite bottom: Some purists might cringe at this motley assortment of equipment operating together for such a frivolous purpose as a steam excursion. What right-thinking railroad would consider stringing together bi-level suburban passenger cars with traditional heavy cars, a gondola, and two new extra-vision cabooses—and have the audacity to haul the incongruous consist with a 4-8-4? Burlington did, and don't you wish you were there? *Richard Jay Solomon*

At Galesburg Railroad Days on May 29, 1992, Burlington Northern displayed extended-vision 12618 painted in patriotic colors along with similarly adorned "Desert Storm" SD60MAC No. 1991, both in support of American troops in Iraq. *Scott Muskopf*

Left and oppposite: On the Oregon Trunk, manned cabooses were still required into the mid-1990s. On July 1, 1994, a BN through freight works its way geographically northward through Willow Creek Canyon toward the Deschutes and Columbia rivers. *Brian Solomon*

In the last light of the day on July 13, 1994, a westward Burlington Northern freight rolls over the old Northern Pacific main line near Rider, North Dakota. At the back is an extended-vision caboose that had become the most common variety of caboose on the late-era BN. The following year the railroad was melded into the Burlington Northern Santa Fe. *Brian Solomon*

In the fading light on July 12, 1994, an empty BN unit coal train heads west through Beach, North Dakota, en route to the Powder River Basin where it will be loaded and sent back out again. *Brian Solomon*

With its back door open to let in the cool mountain breeze, a BN extended-vision caboose trailing a slow eastbound freight provides a stellar view of the Salish Mountains while the train eases to a stop in the Rock Creek siding in northwestern Montana on September 26, 1994. In the distance the faint headlight and silhouette of higher-priority train 46 approaches. *Tom Kline*

Above: Burlington Northern Santa Fe 12555—still in old BN paint—moves west on a ballast train passing Pepin, Wisconsin, in September 2000. *Brian Solomon*

Opposite top: One westward BN freight overtakes another at the yard in Wishram, Washington, in the Columbia River Gorge. At the time of this July 2, 1994, photo BN trains destined for the Oregon Trunk were still using manned cabooses. This photo was taken shortly after the announcement that BN planned to merge with Santa Fe. *Brian Solomon*

Opposite bottom: In case there were any questions as to where this caboose was to be assigned, BN stenciled the information on its side. Among the last places BN regularly assigned cabooses to unit trains was on the former Northern Pacific main line across North Dakota. *Brian Solomon*

Chapter 4

Odds and Ends

Odds and Ends

In twentieth-century North American railway operations, four-wheel railroad equipment was by far the exception rather than the norm. This was not always the case. In the formative days of railway operations all cars tended to be four-wheelers. The development of cars using pairs of four-wheel trucks emerged as a means of improving ride quality and allowing for construction of significantly larger cars. Baltimore & Ohio built two-truck (i.e., eight-wheel) freight cars as early as 1830, but the higher cost of such cars saw many lines continuing to build four-wheelers late into the century.

The most common commercial applications for four-wheel cars were as coal and ore hoppers and for non-revenue cars such as cabooses. Economy-minded railways didn't want to spend any more money than was necessary on cabooses, which, though required for operation of freight trains, didn't add anything to the bottom line. Four-wheel cabooses were commonly known as "bobbers," which reflected their rough ride. It has been suggested that some mean-minded management viewed the rougher ride in the caboose as a means of keeping trainmen

more alert, believing them inclined to doze off on long journeys.

In the 1890s, four-wheel freight cars came to be considered incompatible with new standards requiring automatic couplers and Westinghouse airbrakes; however, some lines continued to acquire four-wheel cabooses. By the early twentieth century, however, four-wheel cabooses were in decline. In some places they were banned for safety reasons (four-wheelers were less stable and had a tendency to turn over in derailments). By mid-century, surviving bobbers were a curiosity, yet as late as the 1950s they could be found on portions of the B&O, on the Rio Grande narrow gauge, and on Lehigh & New England lines in eastern Pennsylvania.

As primitive as bobbers may have been, they weren't the lowliest cabooses ever. One work-a-day caboose that never got as much attention as any of its mainline counterparts—even the bobber—was the transfer caboose. These were Spartan affairs, little more than a box or compartment on a flatcar or frame, yet they provided crews with a safe place to ride. Transfer cabooses were designed for relatively slow-speed freights, such as local trains, yard transfers, and maintenance work, and commonly could be found at major railroad gateways such as Chicago, St. Louis, and Kansas City, where freight cars were interchanged in long blocks. New York Central maintained a substantial fleet of transfer cabooses, which were also favored by terminal railroads such as the Indiana Harbor Belt. Although not pretty to look at, these cars were as much part of the railroad scene as more glamorous cabooses. A few of these curiosities survive today on Amtrak. It might seem incongruous that America's passenger service provider would need cabooses, yet these are retained for maintenance trains on Amtrak's Northeast Corridor.

On many lines cabooses were phased out on mainline freights during the 1980s and 1990s. While through freights today carry just a telemetry device at the back, and crews (reduced in size from five or six men to just two or three) now ride at the head end in the engine cab, many railroads still require cabooses for specific tasks. No longer the pride of the crews that ride in them, these old cars often show their age and decades of hard service. Other cars are well kept, demonstrating their once crucial roles. Some cabooses survive in public parks. Others are owned privately, and a great number can be found preserved on tourist railways and in railroad museums. The heyday of the caboose may have ended decades ago, but the spirit of this stalwart institution survives.

Previous pages:
One of the smallest eight-wheel cabooses to serve a Class 1 American carrier was Kansas City Southern 395, seen here on the Grandview turn at SW Junction in Kansas City, Missouri, on February 7, 1985. Transfer cabooses were typically used only on very short runs, often between yards at big terminals, and didn't offer much more than a safe platform for the conductor or brakeman. *Scott Muskopf*

Above: Lehigh & New England "bobber" 512 rests at Kempton, Pennsylvania. The old four-wheel bobbers were rare in twentieth-century operations, and today only a handful survive. *Brian Solomon*

Opposite top: L&NE operated wooden four-wheel cabooses much later than most other American railroads. L&NE 512 is a classic. Today it survives on the Wanamaker, Kempton, & Southern in Pennsylvania, just over the Blue Ridge from where it once operated. *Brian Solomon*

Opposite bottom: L&NE was used as bridge line from the Maybrook/Campbell Hall, New York, gateway to connections in Eastern Pennsylvania, where it served both anthracite and cement industries. *Brian Solomon*

Above: Baltimore & Ohio four-wheel bobber C1707 was photographed at Spencer, West Virginia, on September 9, 1937. This was one of a dozen four-wheel cars built between 1909 and 1913 for the Coal & Coke Railway Company, a line later acquired by B&O. The cars featured a 13-foot, 6-inch wheelbase and measured just more than 28 feet 4 inches over the coupler faces. They served B&O for decades, although the last were retired by 1954. *Jay Williams collection*

Opposite top: B&O had one of the largest fleets of four-wheel cabooses to survive into the mid-twentieth century. Bobber C1290, pictured at Parkersburg, West Virginia, on February 5, 1934, was of the more common Class K-1 built in the latter part of the nineteenth century. Typically K-1s had an 11-foot wheelbase supporting a wooden body. The top of the cupola was just over 13 feet 11 inches above the rail. *Jay Williams collection*

Opposite bottom: B&O Chicago Terminal C1777 was photographed at State Line Crossing, Indiana, on October 2, 1947. This was among nine four-wheel cabooses built for Buffalo & Susquehanna in the first decade of the twentieth century. B&O acquired B&S in 1932 and designated these cars as Class I-11. Although this example did not feature a cupola, other I-11s did. Sister car C1775 has been preserved at the B&O museum in Baltimore, making it one of only a scant few surviving four-wheel cabooses. *Jay Williams collection*

Above: Riding in early cabooses was perilous. The cause of this accident has been forgotten, but the results were captured on film for posterity. An eastward Boston & Albany freight had derailed in downtown Warren, Massachusetts, in about 1902. B&A four-wheeler No. 5 is on its side, causing great curiosity among the townspeople. Despite the accident, the caboose remained relatively intact. *I. Walter Moore collection, courtesy of Robert A. Buck*

Opposite top: Today we might wonder why seven men posed with this B&A 2-8-0 and four-wheel caboose at Worcester Yard. In the 1890s it was common to find three or more brakemen assigned to a freight. Here, four brakemen are lined up in front of the caboose. Although airbrakes eventually reduced the number of brakemen needed, some railroads continued to operate with five- and six-man crews until the early 1980s. *William Bullard archive, courtesy of Dennis LeBeau*

Opposite bottom: This old Hardwick & Woodbury caboose reveals its heritage with the fading New York Central logo on its side. By the time it was photographed in the late 1930s the Vermont short line had succumbed to the Great Depression and the caboose was among its derelict equipment. *Victor Newton photo, Robert A. Buck collection*

The Rio Grande used bobbers on its narrow gauge lines in Colorado and New Mexico. This little caboose is a rare example of a narrow gauge four-wheeler. Just a handful survive today. *Tom Kline*

A vestige of another era, the ruins of an old Rio Grande caboose sit among the sage near Utah's Soldier's Summit in 1981. *Thomas L. Carver*

A former Rio Grande caboose offered this view on a Cumbres & Toltec photo freight excursion near Los Pinos, Colorado, on September 27, 1999. *Tom Kline*

Above: The diminutive nature of this old Colorado & Southern bobber has endeared it to enthusiasts and ensured its preservation. It now resides at the Colorado Railroad Museum in Golden, Colorado. *Tom Kline*

Opposite top: C&S four-wheeler 1006 was photographed in this mountain setting at Silver Plume, Colorado, in about 1946. *The Sirman Collection*

Opposite bottom: A rare photo depicts Pennsylvania Railroad 3-foot-gauge four-wheeler 1001 bouncing along on a Waynesburg & Washington mixed train in the late 1930s. *Vic Newton photo, Robert A. Buck collection*

Above: Seen at Attica, New York, on May 2, 1987, Conrail Class N8b No. 23540 began life as a New Haven Railroad NE-5 built by Pullman-Standard. Penn Central converted it from a cupola design to an ad hoc bay-window type. The white dot next to the number indicates it is suitable in helper service ahead of pushers. *Brian Solomon*

Opposite top: Conrail 23625 is another example of an old cupola caboose transformed with add-on bay-windows. It is working a Conrail run-through freight to Chicago & North Western via the Indiana Harbor Belt and is seen here passing Blue Island, Illinois, on the Ides of March 1980. *Scott Muskopf*

Opposite bottom: Some steel mill and terminal railroads built cabooses from old steam engine tenders. This adaptive reuse of rolling stock resulted in many distinctive-looking cabooses on such railroads as the Monongahela Connecting and Union Railroad. Perhaps the largest fleet of cabooses built from recycled components belonged to the Lackawanna. *David Hamley photo, Patrick Yough collection*

Penn Central Class N11E No. 18598 was built by DS Incorporated at the old New York Central Despatch Shops in East Rochester, New York. In March 1971 it displays fresh Penn Central green paint at Harmon, New York. Although PC's locomotives wore black paint, its cabooses were more attractively adorned. *George W. Kowanski*

In October 1987, a Conrail local works east on the former New York Central main line with Class N9 transfer caboose 18393 bringing up the rear. Although Spartan, Conrail's transfer cabooses provided crews with necessary shelter on short runs. In the foreground is the old New York, West Shore & Buffalo, a short portion of which Conrail used as a bypass around Rochester. *Brian Solomon*

Painted in safety orange, Amtrak 14032 survives for use on maintenance-of-way trains on the Northeast Corridor. It is based out of the old Cedar Hill Yard in New Haven, Connecticut. Now 40 years old, the old N-11 transfer caboose was built for Penn Central in 1970 by Despatch Shops in East Rochester, New York. *Brian Solomon*

In 2003, Chicago Short Line became the South Chicago & Indiana Harbor Railway. On November 10, 2005, the railroad's local freight waits with transfer caboose No. 5, originally an Elgin, Joliet & Eastern car, for clearance to enter Norfolk Southern's Chicago line near River Branch Junction in South Chicago. *Thomas Figura*

Scranton-based Delaware Lackawanna is operated by Genesee Valley Transportation and serves former Delaware & Hudson and Delaware, Lackawanna & Western trackage in eastern Pennsylvania. On October 1, 1996, DL's recently acquired former CP Rail M630 leads a second-hand transfer caboose on the old D&H main line north of its Scranton, Pennsylvania, yard. *Brian Solomon*

Chicago Short Line transfer caboose No. 5 navigates industrial trackage across 106th Street to reach Bayou Steel on January 2, 1995. CSL continued to employ this traditional caboose because of the numerous long reverse moves made by its local freights. *Brian Solomon*

Above: Davenport, Rock Island & Northwestern Railway transfer caboose No. 2 makes a reverse move at West Davenport, Iowa, on July 15, 1982. *John Leopard*

Opposite top: Manufacturers Railway Company's smartly painted transfer caboose No. 514 sits in the snow at St. Louis, Missouri, on December 22, 1983. *Scott Muskopf*

Opposite bottom: On September 19, 1981, an Illinois Central Gulf transfer caboose rests at Venice, Illinois. Many transfer cabooses were built on the frames of old freight cars. *Scott Muskopf*

On February 22, 2010, CSX 904106 made a rare appearance at Palmer, Massachusetts, at the back of a welded rail train. Built as part of Chessie System's final caboose order in 1980, this survivor is now in its thirtieth year of service. *Brian Solomon*

As built, this Fruit Growers Express design measured just under 41 feet 8 inches long between coupler faces. The caboose body, excluding awnings over the end platforms, is just over 30 feet. *Brian Solomon*

The main body of Class C-27A is 8 feet 5¾ inches wide, while the outside dimensions of the bay-window measure 10 feet 7¼ inches. Originally, CSX had 94 cabooses of this type. Today only a handful remains active. *Brian Solomon*

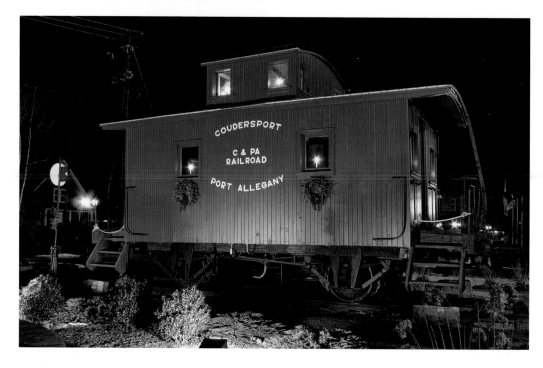

A preserved Coudersport & Port Allegheny four-wheel bobber basks in the lights near the old railway station at Coudersport, Pennsylvania. Buffalo & Susquehanna's shops at nearby Galeton built this antique early in the twentieth century. B&S operated a small fleet of four-wheel cabooses. *Brian Solomon*

Although four-wheel freight cars were standard practice in the early days of American railroading, by 1900 railway cars with four-wheel trucks at both ends were standard. The exception on some lines was with cabooses, which continued to be built as traditional four-wheelers. *Brian Solomon*

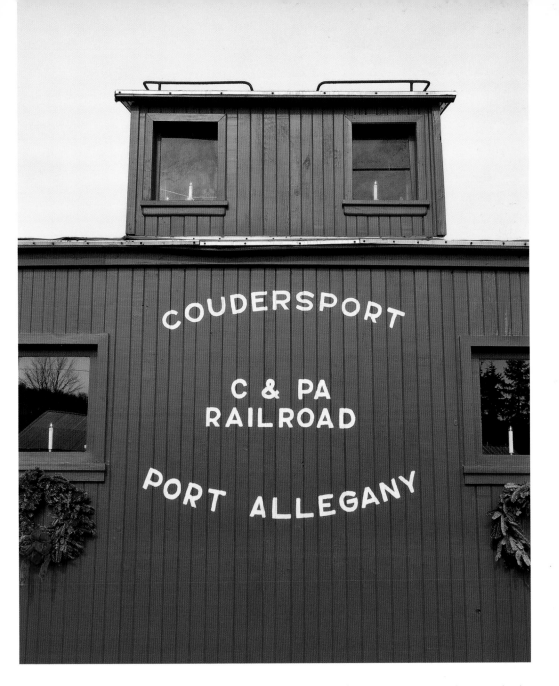

Built in 1882 as a narrow gauge line, Coudersport & Port Allegheny was converted to standard gauge six years later. In 1964, the Wellsville, Addison & Galeton's owners acquired the C&PA, operating it for just a few years. Abandonment came in 1970. This caboose is one of the last surviving remnants of the defunct line. *Brian Solomon*

Pioneer Valley Railroad's C457R has special duty at the back of an August 2007 excursion over the length of the railroad from Westfield to Holyoke, Massachusetts, celebrating the company's 25th anniversary. Normally the caboose is used primarily as a shoving platform for long reverse moves. *Brian Solomon*

Pioneer Valley's car is a former Boston & Maine caboose similar to those pictured in Chapter 1. Dave Swirk, a supervisor with the railroad, explains that they use it as a shoving platform and for excursions. *Brian Solomon*

The cupola arrangement of Pioneer Valley C457. The high perch gives railroaders a good view of their train. *Brian Solomon*

This classic tilt-board signal protected Genesee & Wyoming's crossing with the old New York Central Peanut Line at P&L Junction near Caledonia, New York. This view looks west on the Peanut from the back of a G&W caboose. *Brian Solomon*